Amphibians & Reptiles

Grades 1–3

Project Manager:
Thad H. McLaurin

Writer:
Jennifer Overend Prior

Editors:
Njeri Legrand, Jennifer Munnerlyn, Sue Walker

Art Coordinator:
Clevell Harris

Artists:
Pam Crane, Clevell Harris, Susan Hodnett,
Greg D. Rieves, Rebecca Saunders

Cover Artists:
Nick Greenwood and Kimberly Richard

www.themailbox.com

©2000 by THE EDUCATION CENTER, INC.
All rights reserved.
ISBN #1-56234-365-3

Manufactured in the United States
10 9 8 7 6 5 4 3 2 1

Table of Contents

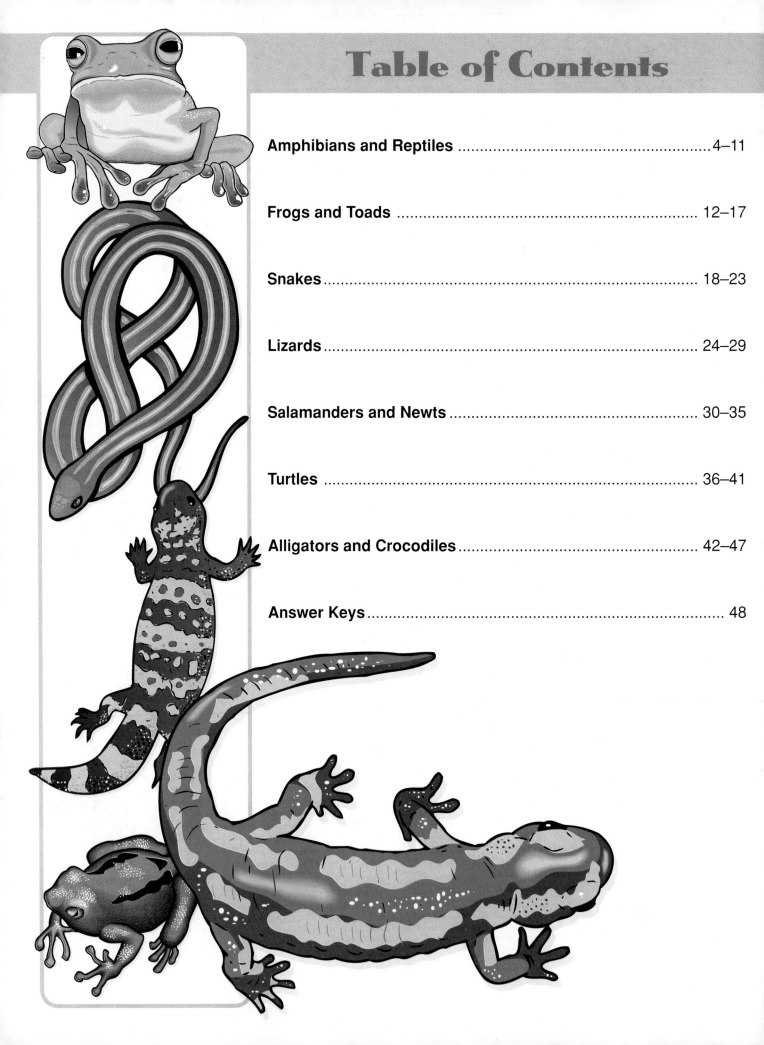

About This Book

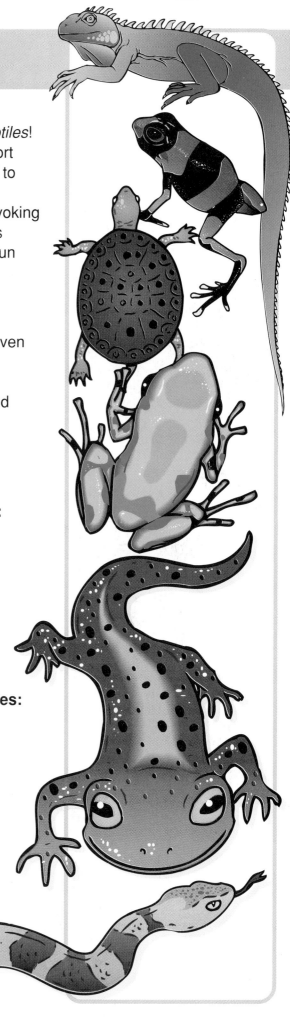

Welcome to *Investigating Science—Amphibians and Reptiles*! This book is one of ten must-have resource books that support the National Science Education Standards and are designed to supplement and enhance your existing science curriculum. Packed with practical cross-curricular ideas and thought-provoking reproducibles, these all-new, content-specific resource books provide primary teachers with a collection of innovative and fun activities for teaching thematic science units.

Included in this book:

Investigating Science—Amphibians and Reptiles contains seven cross-curricular thematic units each containing
- Background information for the teacher
- Easy-to-implement instructions for science experiments and projects
- Student-centered activities and reproducibles
- Literature links

Cross-curricular thematic units found in this book:
- *Amphibians and Reptiles*
- *Frogs and Toads*
- *Snakes*
- *Lizards*
- *Salamanders and Newts*
- *Turtles*
- *Alligators and Crocodiles*

Other books in the primary Investigating Science series:
- *Investigating Science—Environment*
- *Investigating Science—Insects*
- *Investigating Science—Solar System*
- *Investigating Science—Plants*
- *Investigating Science—Energy*
- *Investigating Science—Mammals*
- *Investigating Science—Weather*
- *Investigating Science—Rocks & Minerals*
- *Investigating Science—Health & Safety*

Amphibians and Reptiles

Use this collection of creative activities to excite your students as they discover and explore the differences between amphibians and reptiles.

Crazy Chameleons
(Reading, Art, Writing)

Use this activity to introduce your students to an amazing reptile, the chameleon. Explain to your children that a chameleon is a special reptile that can change its skin color to blend with its surroundings. If possible, show the class a photograph of a chameleon. Then introduce your students to an even more amazing chameleon by reading Eric Carle's *The Mixed-Up Chameleon* (HarperTrophy, 1988). The chameleon in this book lives in a zoo and can not only change colors, but it can also take on characteristics of other animals at the zoo. After reading the story aloud, give each child a sheet of drawing paper and crayons. Have each student think about the different characteristics of reptiles and which ones he'd like to take on. Then have each child draw a picture of himself with the additional reptilian characteristics. Also have the child write a few sentences telling why he chose these particular characteristics. Culminate the activity by having each child share his drawing and writing with the rest of the class. Then post all the drawings on a board titled "Crazy Reptilian Chameleons."

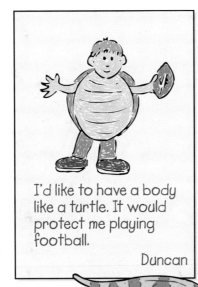

I'd like to have a body like a turtle. It would protect me playing football.

Duncan

Background for the Teacher

Amphibians and Reptiles…
- are vertebrates (have backbones)
- are cold-blooded animals
- are mostly meat eaters

Amphibians…
- have no hair, feathers, or scales on their skin
- breathe through their lungs, breathe through their skin, or both
- need freshwater to keep their skin moist and some need a watery environment in order to reproduce
- are divided into three groups: frogs and toads; newts, salamanders, and sirens; and caecilians (wormlike creatures)

Reptiles...
- evolved from amphibians
- lay eggs on land or bear live young on land
- are covered with protective horny scales or plates
- have four legs, except for snakes and some lizards that have no legs at all
- have lungs
- hibernate in cold winter weather
- are divided into four groups: lizards and snakes, turtles and tortoises, crocodilians, and tuatara (a lizardlike reptile, in its own group, that is the oldest species of reptile)

"Toad-ally" Cool Amphibian/ Reptilian Booklist

About Reptiles: A Guide for Children by Cathryn Sill (Peachtree Publishers, Ltd.; 1999)
Eyewitness Books: Amphibian by Dr. Barry Clarke (Alfred A. Knopf, Inc.; 1993)
Eyewitness Books: Reptile by Colin McCarthy (Alfred A. Knopf, Inc.; 1991)
I Can Read About Reptiles™ by David Cutts (Troll Associates, Inc.; 1997)
National Audubon Society First Field Guide: Amphibians by Brian Cassie (Scholastic Inc., 1999)
National Audubon Society First Field Guide: Reptiles by John L. Behler (Scholastic Inc., 1999)
What Is a Reptile? by Bobbie Kalman (Crabtree Publishing, 1999)
The Yucky Reptile Alphabet Book by Jerry Pallotta (Charlesbridge Publishing Company, Inc.; 1990)

Investigation Logs
(Research, Making a Field Guide)

For additional reinforcement of the unique characteristics of amphibians and reptiles, use this cool classroom amphibian and reptile field guide idea. Have each student research a desired amphibian or reptile, or, if desired, assign each student a particular amphibian or reptile to research. Supply each student with crayons and a copy of "Investigation Log" on page 7. Instruct each student to complete the reproducible as directed. (Younger students may need your assistance in researching and filling out their logs.) When your students have completed the activity, provide time for them to share their investigation logs and drawings with their classmates. Then compile the illustrated logs into one book titled "Our Classroom Amphibian & Reptilian Field Guide." (For durability, laminate each page before compiling into a book.) Each night send the classroom field guide home with a different student to share with her family.

Name **Freddy** — Research

Investigation Log

Draw and color a picture of your animal in its habitat. Write the name of the animal on the line.

Bullfrog

Complete these sentences about your animal.

1. My animal lives in __the United States, Canada, and Mexico__.
2. My animal eats __fish, mice, snakes, and small frogs__.
3. My animal moves with __strong back legs that help it jump__.
4. My animal's body is covered with __dull green skin and it has a yellow or white belly__.
5. Interesting facts about my animal: __Its back legs can be up to ten inches long. It likes to live in ponds and lakes. A female can lay 10,000 eggs.__

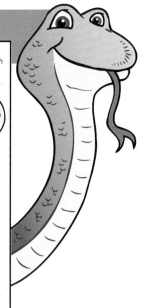

Who Am I?

Rayna

I am a reptile.
I live in Florida.
My skin is like armor.
I can be 19 feet long.
I have lots of teeth.
Who am I?

Who Am I?
(Research, Writing, Art)

Have students demonstrate their knowledge about amphibians and reptiles with this unique activity. Each child will need a large sheet of construction paper divided into thirds (as shown), a piece of writing paper, and crayons or markers. Have each student choose a different amphibian or reptile and then write three or more clues about the animal on her writing paper. Each youngster then glues the clues to the bottom third of her construction paper and illustrates a picture of the animal in the middle. Next, she folds down the top third of her paper and adds the title "Who Am I?" Provide time for each student to share her clues with classmates, revealing the picture when it is guessed correctly. Post each student's work on a bulletin board titled "Who Am I?" so that visitors can read the clues and then lift the flaps to check their guesses.

Lizard Licked!
(Matching Game)

Chameleon
Skin color changes to its surroundings

Chameleon
Skin color changes to its surroundings

Tuata...
Called the... fossil" bec... hasn't cha... millions o...

Tuatara
Called the "living fossil" because it hasn't changed in millions of years

To culminate your study of reptiles, have your students play a game of Lizard Licked! This game is similar to Go Fish, except students try to collect pairs of reptiles to win the game. To prepare for the game, duplicate two tagboard copies of the cards on page 8 for each group of two players. (If desired, have students color the illustrated cards before cutting them apart.) To play, one student deals seven cards to herself and seven to the other player; then she places the remaining cards facedown to form a draw pile. Each player places all her matching pairs of reptiles on the table. Player 1 begins by asking Player 2 for a card to match one that she is holding. If she receives the match from Player 2, she places the pair on the table and takes another turn. If Player 2 does not have the card Player 1 requested, Player 2 says "Lizard Licked," and Player 1 draws a card from the pile. If she does not draw a match, she keeps the card and Player 2 takes a turn. Anytime a player lays her last cards on the table, she takes one card from the draw pile. When the draw pile is gone, the game ends. The player with the most pairs wins the game. After each pair completes its game, store the cards in a resealable plastic bag and place them in a learning center for students to use in their free time. Be prepared—they'll want to be lizard licked again and again!

Amphibians

Tree Toad

Tiger Salamander

African Bullfrog

Reptiles

Gila Monster

Western Diamondback Rattlesnake

All Sorts of Fun With Amphibians and Reptiles!
(Sorting)

After learning about the differences between amphibians and reptiles, challenge your students to this sorting activity. Tape two large sheets of chart paper to the wall; then label one sheet "Amphibians" and the other sheet "Reptiles." Next, make one copy each of pages 9 and 10. (If desired, enlarge the illustrations.) Separate the illustrations into separate cards by cutting along the bold lines. Then place all of the illustrations into a paper bag. Have each child draw one illustration from the bag. Tell the student to study the illustration carefully and try to determine whether it's an amphibian or a reptile based on its name and the way it looks. Then, one at a time, have each student tape his animal illustration onto the appropriate sheet of chart paper. Culminate the activity by discussing as a class what makes each animal an amphibian or a reptile. *(See answer key on page 48.)*

Investigation Log

Draw and color a picture of your animal in its habitat.
Write the name of the animal on the line.

_____

Complete these sentences about your animal.

1. My animal lives in _____.

2. My animal eats _____.

3. My animal moves with _____.

4. My animal's body is covered with _____.

5. Interesting facts about my animal: _____

   _____

   _____

   _____

Patterns

Use with "Lizard Licked!" on page 6.

Tuatara
Called the "living fossil" because it hasn't changed in millions of years

Giant Galapagos Tortoise
A giant land tortoise that weighs around 500 pounds

American Alligator
The biggest reptile in North America

Garter Snake
The most common snake in the United States

Western Diamondback Rattlesnake
Uses the rattle at the end of its tail as a warning signal

Leatherback Turtle
Has leatherlike skin instead of a hard shell and can weigh 1,500 pounds

Flying Dragon
Uses winglike flaps of skin to glide through the air

Rough Green Snake
A tree climber; likes vegetation along lakes

Gila monster
One of the few venomous reptiles in the world

Chameleon
Skin color changes to its surroundings

Gila Monster	**Tree Toad**	**Western Diamondback Rattlesnake**	**Tiger Salamander**
Green Tree Frog	**Tuatara**	**European Common Frog**	**Leatherback Turtle**
Giant Galapagos Tortoise	**Marine Toad**	**Gecko**	**Fire Salamander**

Patterns

Use with "All Sorts of Fun With Amphibians and Reptiles!" on page 6.

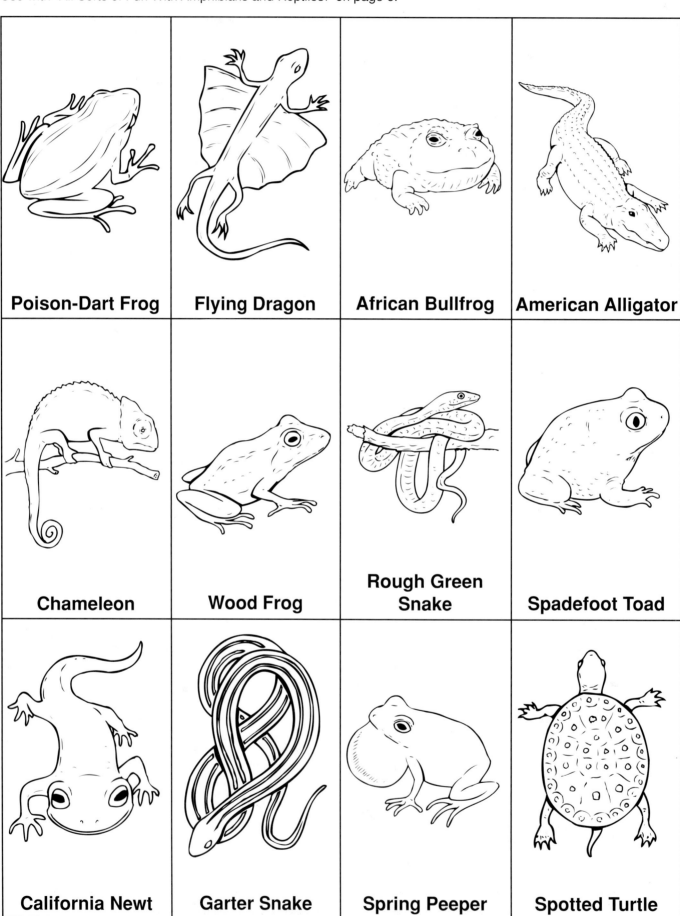

Poison-Dart Frog	**Flying Dragon**	**African Bullfrog**	**American Alligator**
Chameleon	**Wood Frog**	**Rough Green Snake**	**Spadefoot Toad**
California Newt	**Garter Snake**	**Spring Peeper**	**Spotted Turtle**

Compare and Contrast	Amphibians	Reptiles
How do they breathe?		
Where do they live?		
How do they move?		
What do they eat?		
Do they need to be in or near water?		
Do they lay eggs?		

Note to the teacher: Use this page as a research activity or as an assessment to check students' learning.

Frogs and Toads

This "toad-ally" awesome collection of ideas and reproducibles is sure to enhance your study of frogs and toads!

"Pond-ering" About Frogs and Toads
(Research Skills)

As you jump into your study of frogs and toads, your youngsters are sure to have plenty of questions about these amazing amphibians. Use these questions to create an interactive bulletin board perfect for reinforcing students' research skills. To make the board, mount large frog and lily pad cutouts (see patterns on page 15) to the center of a bulletin board that's covered in blue paper. Next, place pushpins (one for each student in your class) all around the large frog cutout, and title the board "Check Out My Pad." Then duplicate the lily pad pattern onto green construction paper to make a class supply. Give each student one lily pad. Instruct her to write one question about frogs or toads on it and then punch a hole at the top of the cutout. Place the completed cutouts in a container near the board along with a supply of nonfiction books about frogs and toads. During free time or center time, instruct each student to select a lily pad cutout from the container, read the question, and research to find the answer. Then have the child record the answer on the lily pad and hang it on one of the pushpins for all to read and learn more about frogs and toads.

Background for the Teacher

Frogs and Toads…
- can be found living almost anywhere in the world, except where it is very cold.
- (most) begin life as eggs in water, hatch into tadpoles, and then develop into adult frogs or toads that are ready to come out of the water.
- use their long, sticky tongues to catch prey, such as worms, snails, and insects.

Frogs…
- have moist, smooth skin.
- have small teeth on their upper jaw for holding prey.
- do not have bumps on their heads.
- can jump several times the length of their bodies.
- lay their eggs in clumps.

Toads…
- have plump bodies.
- have dry, warty skin.
- have a large poison gland behind each "ear" (tympani).
- hop only a few inches at a time.
- lay their eggs in strings.

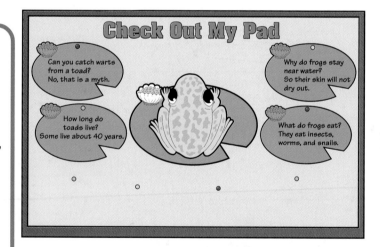

Check Out My Pad

Can you catch warts from a toad? No, that is a myth.

Why do frogs stay near water? So their skin will not dry out.

How long do toads live? Some live about 40 years.

What do frogs eat? They eat insects, worms, and snails.

Leaping Literature Links

All-Weather Friends by Udo Weigelt (North-South Books Inc., 1999)

Frogs and Toads by Bobbie Kalman (Crabtree Publishing Company, 1994)

From Frog to Tadpole by Wendy Pfeffer (Harper-Collins Children's Books, 1994)

Grandpa Toad's Secrets by Keiko Kasza (The Putnam Publishing Group, 1998)

Tale of a Tadpole by Barbara Anne Porte (Orchard Books, 1997)

"Toad-ally" Awesome Tales
(Creative Writing)

Oh, no! It's raining frogs!

The toad and the magic toadstool

Have youngsters leap into creative writing with this awesome activity! Make five copies of the frog pattern on page 15 on green construction paper. Next, cut out each frog and program it with one of the five prompts shown in the box. Then place the programmed frogs in a large envelope. At the beginning of the week, explain to your youngsters that over the years people have made up many tales and superstitions about frogs and toads, such as that frogs can predict the weather, frogs fall from the sky during rain, and you can catch warts from a toad. Then have a student select a prompt from the envelope and read it aloud to the class. Instruct each student to write a story that focuses on the prompt. Continue this process each day of the week with a different prompt. At the end of the week, allow each student to read her favorite tale to the rest of the class. If desired, compile the completed stories into a book titled "Fabulous Froggy Tales!"

Writing Prompts
- Oh, no! It's raining frogs!
- The frog that wanted to become a prince
- How the toad lost its warts
- One day my frog predicted the weather!
- The toad and the magic toadstool

How the toad lost its warts

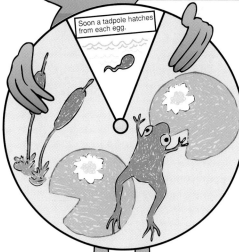
Soon a tadpole hatches from each egg.

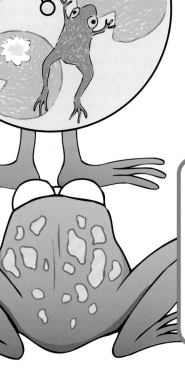

From Egg to Frog
(Sequencing, Reading Comprehension, Art)

To explore the development of a frog, read *Frogs* by Gail Gibbons (Holiday House, Inc.; 1994) to your students. Follow up the reading of this informative book by guiding your students through the steps below to create life cycle picture wheels of a frog. When these "ribbit-ing" projects are complete, have each youngster take his project home to teach family members and friends all about a frog's unique life cycle!

Materials for each student:
1 white construction paper copy of page 16
1 blank, white construction paper circle cut the same size as the wheel
  pattern on page 16 with one triangular section cut away
1 brad
crayons
scissors
glue

Steps:
1. Cut out the wheel pattern and information cards.
2. Read the cards carefully. Lay them in order on your desk.
3. Glue the cards in order onto the gray boxes around the wheel pattern.
4. Beneath each card, draw and color a picture to match the card.
5. On one side of the blank wheel, draw and color a frog habitat.
6. Place the wheel containing the information cards underneath the wheel with the frog habitat illustration.
7. Insert a brad through the center of both wheels.
8. Slowly turn the wheel and read about the development of a frog.

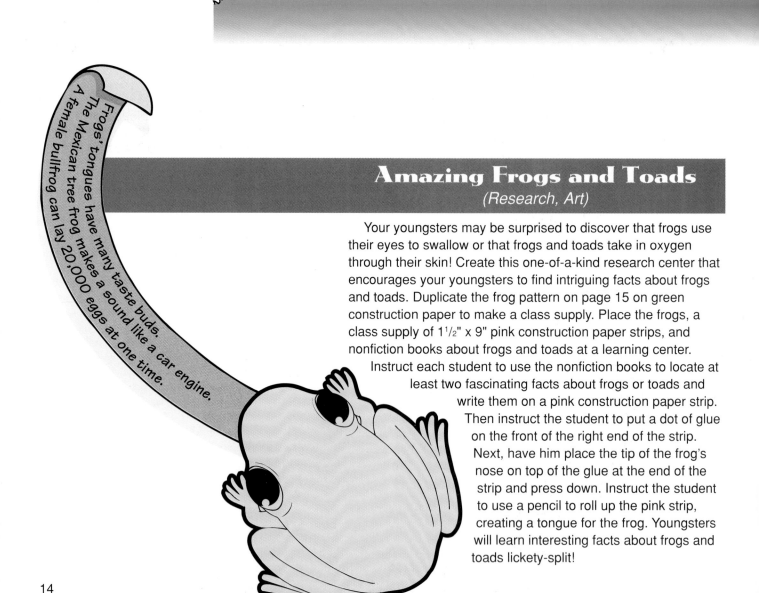

Hiding Out
(Creative Thinking, Art)

Give students a close-up on camouflage with this creative-thinking activity. Explain to youngsters that frogs and toads are eaten by animals such as snakes, birds, and even other frogs! Share the story *How to Hide a Meadow Frog & Other Amphibians* by Ruth Heller (Grosset & Dunlap, Publishers; 1995) to help students understand that the colors of some frogs and toads help *camouflage,* or hide, them from these predators. Provide each student with a copy of the frog pattern on page 15. Then instruct each student to select an area of the classroom—such as a desk, the carpeting, or the wall— where he can hide his frog. Have each student color his frog to match the selected area. Then have him cut out the frog and use tape to mount it in that area. Challenge classroom visitors to find these hidden frogs and toads!

Frogs' tongues have many taste buds. The Mexican tree frog makes a sound like a car engine. A female bullfrog can lay 20,000 eggs at one time.

Amazing Frogs and Toads
(Research, Art)

Your youngsters may be surprised to discover that frogs use their eyes to swallow or that frogs and toads take in oxygen through their skin! Create this one-of-a-kind research center that encourages your youngsters to find intriguing facts about frogs and toads. Duplicate the frog pattern on page 15 on green construction paper to make a class supply. Place the frogs, a class supply of 1 1/2" x 9" pink construction paper strips, and nonfiction books about frogs and toads at a learning center. Instruct each student to use the nonfiction books to locate at least two fascinating facts about frogs or toads and write them on a pink construction paper strip. Then instruct the student to put a dot of glue on the front of the right end of the strip. Next, have him place the tip of the frog's nose on top of the glue at the end of the strip and press down. Instruct the student to use a pencil to roll up the pink strip, creating a tongue for the frog. Youngsters will learn interesting facts about frogs and toads lickety-split!

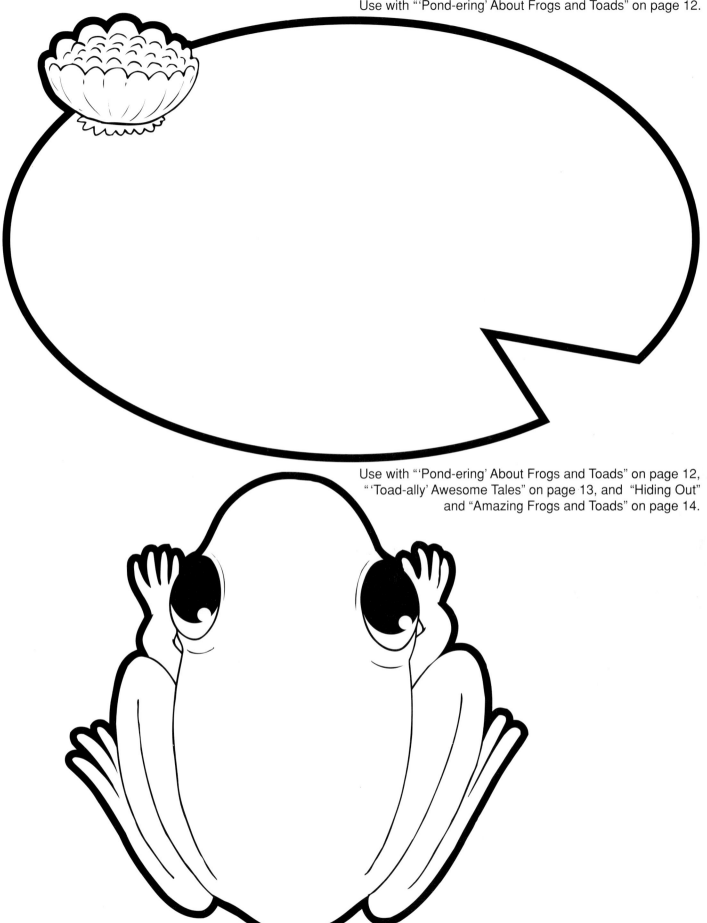

Use with "'Pond-ering' About Frogs and Toads" on page 12,
"'Toad-ally' Awesome Tales" on page 13, and "Hiding Out"
and "Amazing Frogs and Toads" on page 14.

Patterns

Use with "From Egg to Frog" on page 13.

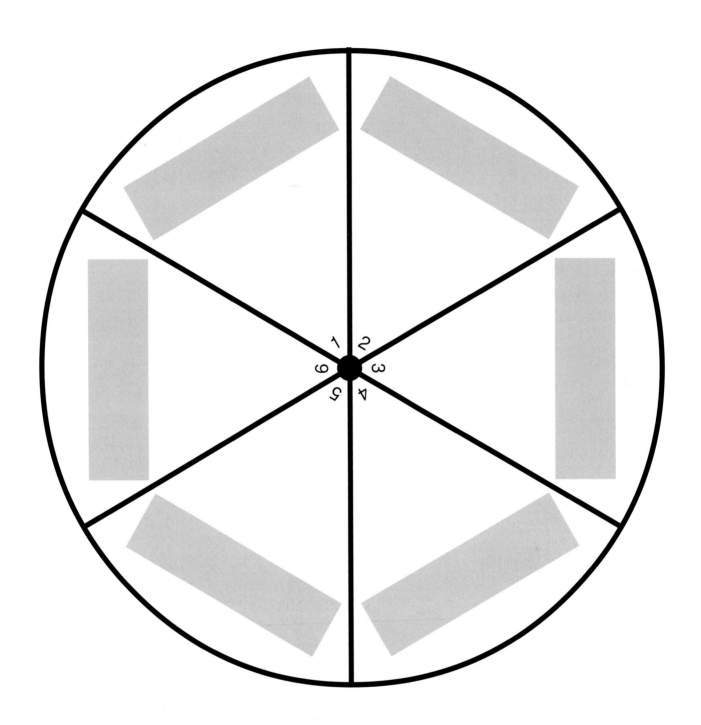

Information Cards

A female frog lays eggs in the pond.	Soon a tadpole hatches from each egg.	First, the tadpole's back legs begin to sprout.
Next, the front legs start to appear.	Then the tail starts to disappear.	Now a frog is ready to come out of the water.

Name _____

How Do Frogs and Toads Measure Up?

Frogs and toads come in many different sizes.
Read about each frog or toad.
Then find an item that is the same length.
Write the name of the item on the line.

The paradoxical frog grows backwards! It shrinks from a large tadpole down to a 2-inch frog.

The goliath frog is the largest of all frogs. This frog may grow to 12 inches long!

The chirping frog makes a sound like a cricket's chirp. This frog can grow to 1 1/2 inches long.

The Cuban arrow-poison frog is the smallest of all frogs. This frog only grows to about 1/2 inch long!

Bullfrogs take about 5 years to become adults. These frogs can grow to 8 inches long.

The giant toad is one of the largest toads! It can grow to 9 inches long.

Leopard frogs have many spots! They can grow to 4 inches long.

Tree frogs are usually excellent jumpers. These tiny frogs only grow to about 1 inch long.

The Surinam toad does not have a tongue! This unique frog can grow to 8 inches long.

©2000 The Education Center, Inc. • Investigating Science • Amphibians and Reptiles • TEC1741

SNAKES

Wind your way through a sensational study of snakes with this super collection of activities and reproducibles.

Busy Bodies
(Snake Anatomy)

Snakes have fascinating features from head to tail! Use this fact-sharing idea to help your youngsters learn more about the bodies of these slithery creatures. Mount a large snake cutout (see pattern on page 21) in a prominent classroom location. Next, cut eight colorful sentence strips to resemble snakes. Then write each fact below onto a separate snake-shaped sentence strip. Each day post one snake-fact strip underneath the large snake pattern. Then read aloud and discuss the fact with your class. After all eight facts are posted, encourage students to continue to find additional snake anatomy facts to add to the display.

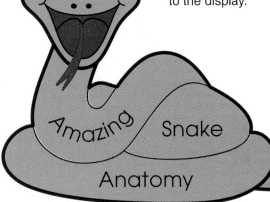

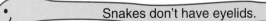

- Snakes don't have eyelids.
- Snakes smell with their tongues.
- Most snakes have sharp, slender teeth to grab prey.
- Snakes can swallow prey whole.
- Snakes are covered with dry, scaly skin.
- A snake's coloring often matches its surroundings.
- Snakes *molt,* or shed their skin.
- Snakes have sculls, vertebrae, and ribs.

Background for the Teacher

- There are over 2,500 different kinds of snakes.
- Snakes can be found in deserts, forests, and seas.
- Most snakes live in warm areas, but a few, such as the Old World viper, may be found above the Arctic Circle.
- Only about 300 species of snakes are poisonous.
- Some snakes use *constriction* to immobilize their prey; they squeeze the animal and prevent it from breathing.
- Most snakes eat a variety of animals, such as birds, fish, frogs, lizards, and small rodents. Snakes, such as the Asian king cobras and North American king snakes, even eat other snakes!
- Snakes eat only about once every two weeks.

Snaky Literature Selections

Amazing Snakes by Alexandra Parsons (Knopf, 1990)

Hide and Snake by Keith Baker (Harcourt Brace & Company, 1995)

How Snake Got His Hiss by Marguerite W. Davol (Orchard Books, 1996)

Outside and Inside Snakes by Sandra Markle (Atheneum Books for Young Readers, 1998)

Verdi by Janell Cannon (Harcourt Brace & Company, 1997)

Snake Eyes
(Arts and Crafts)

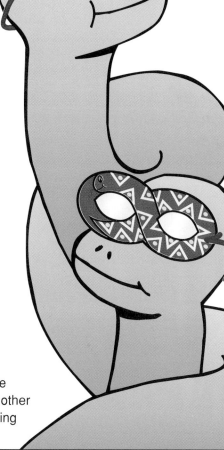

Give your youngsters insight on snakes' eyesight with this one-of-a-kind art project. Explain to your youngsters that instead of eyelids, snakes have clear protective scales that cover their eyes. Next, tell your students that some *diurnal* snakes—snakes active during the day—have built-in sunglasses! Explain that their eyes have yellow-tinted lenses that reduce the sun's glare. Have each youngster make his very own pair of diurnal snake eyes! Distribute the materials and guide each student through the steps listed below.

Materials for each student: 1 colored construction paper copy of the mask pattern on page 21; another sheet of construction paper (same color); scissors; pencil; two 3" squares cut from yellow cellophane; glue; two 1' lengths of yarn; crayons, markers, or various craft supplies; hole puncher

Steps:
1. Cut out the mask pattern. *(Provide assistance with cutting the eyeholes if needed.)*
2. Trace the pattern onto another sheet of construction paper and cut out.
3. Place each cutout on your work surface. *(The programmed pattern should be faceup.)*
4. Dot glue around each eyehole of the blank pattern, place a cellophane square over each hole, and press the cellophane in place. Dot glue around the outer edges of the pattern.
5. Place the programmed pattern (still faceup) directly on top of the blank pattern.
6. Use crayons, markers, or other craft supplies to decorate the programmed pattern.
7. Hole-punch the left and right sides of the mask where indicated. Thread one end of a length of yarn through a hole and tie. Repeat the process with the other length of yarn and the other hole. Then secure the mask to your head by tying the two loose ends together at the back of your head.

Good Vibrations
(Experiment)

All ears—that's what your youngsters will be as they learn about how snakes hear sound! Explain to students that snakes do not have ears to hear sound that travels through the air. Further explain that snakes pick up sound by detecting vibrations that travel through the ground or through water. Tell youngsters that sound occurs when something moves or vibrates and that snakes feel the vibrations of sound instead of hearing it. Use the following activity to help students understand how vibration and sound are related. Provide each student with a rubber band. Then have each student stretch her rubber band between two fingers and pluck it with her free hand. Ask your students if the rubber band made a sound. *(Yes.)* Then ask if they could "feel" the sound the rubber band made. *(Yes.)* Explain to your students that the sound they "felt" was the vibration made by the rubber band. Then explain that feeling this sound is similar to the way snakes experience sound.

Winding Down
(Assessment)

Wind down your study of snakes with this "ssssu-per" assessment activity. First, provide each student with the materials listed. Then guide the student through the steps provided to make a snake booklet like the one shown. Once each student has assembled his booklet, have him write what he has learned about each topic on the corresponding booklet page. Students will be "sssssur-prised" at just how much they've learned!

Materials for each student: 1 tan, yellow, or green construction paper copy of the booklet pages on page 23; pencil; scissors; glue; one 2" square of red construction paper

Steps:
1. Cut out each strip of booklet pages along the bold lines.
2. Align the two strips end to end and glue them together where indicated.
3. Using the thin lines as guides, accordion-fold the project so that the booklet cover is on top and the remaining pages are beneath it.
4. Cut out a snake's tongue from the red construction paper square. Dot glue on the cover where indicated and attach the tongue to the snake's mouth.
5. Write your name on the back cover of the booklet.

Step 2

Step 3

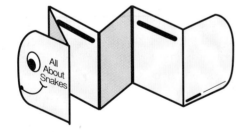

Completed Project

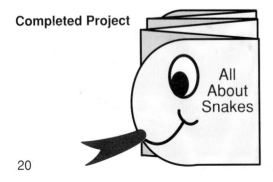

Getting the Scoop on Snakes
(Listening Skills, Making an Info Booklet)

Reinforce your youngsters' listening skills and introduce them to six different kinds of fascinating snakes with this info booklet project. Provide each student with the materials below; then guide her through each step to create her info booklet.

Materials: 1 white construction paper copy of page 22, six 4½" x 6" rectangles of construction paper, one 6" x 9" rectangle of construction paper, scissors, crayons, stapler, glue

Steps:
1. Have each student cut out the cards on page 22 along the bold lines. Then read each description card aloud and ask her to color the snake that is being described.
2. Next, have the student pair each colored snake card with its matching description card.
3. Instruct the student to glue each pair of cards onto a 4½" x 6" rectangle of construction paper. While the glue is drying, have her fold a 6" x 9" sheet of construction paper in half to make a booklet cover.
4. Direct the student to stack her booklet pages, slip them inside the folded booklet cover, and staple along the fold.
5. Instruct the student to title her booklet "Splendid Snakes," write her name on the cover, and decorate the cover with illustrations of snakes.

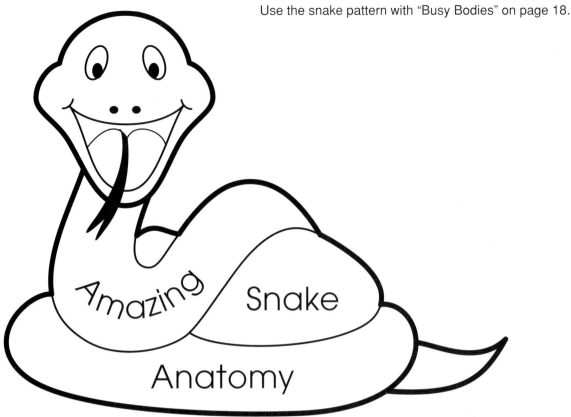

Use the mask pattern with "Snake Eyes" on page 19.

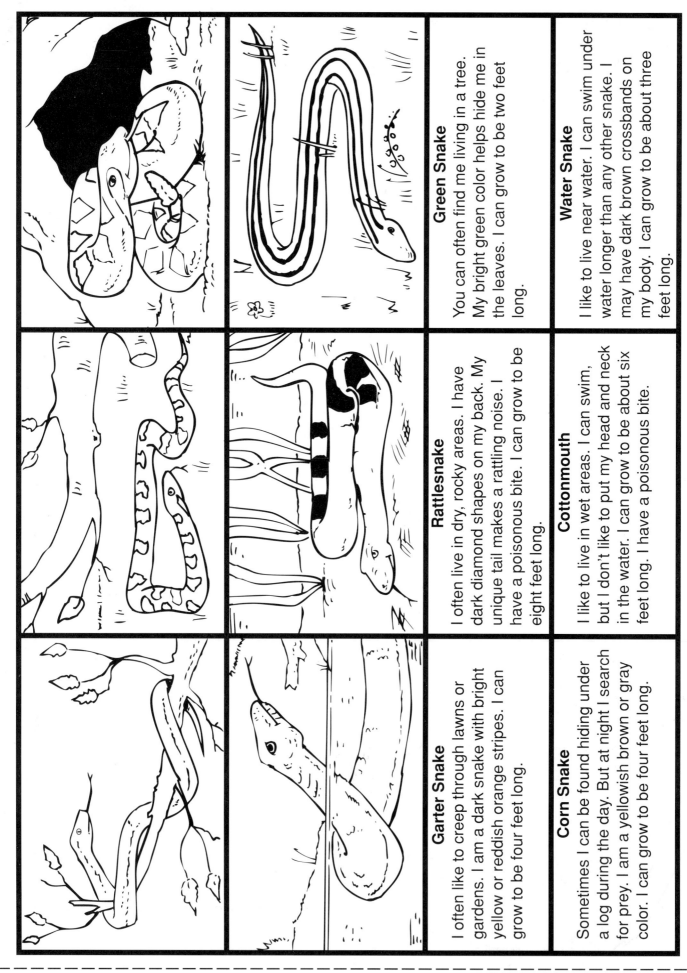

Green Snake

You can often find me living in a tree. My bright green color helps hide me in the leaves. I can grow to be two feet long.

Water Snake

I like to live near water. I can swim under water longer than any other snake. I may have dark brown crossbands on my body. I can grow to be about three feet long.

Rattlesnake

I often live in dry, rocky areas. I have dark diamond shapes on my back. My unique tail makes a rattling noise. I have a poisonous bite. I can grow to be eight feet long.

Cottonmouth

I like to live in wet areas. I can swim, but I don't like to put my head and neck in the water. I can grow to be about six feet long. I have a poisonous bite.

Garter Snake

I often like to creep through lawns or gardens. I am a dark snake with bright yellow or reddish orange stripes. I can grow to be four feet long.

Corn Snake

Sometimes I can be found hiding under a log during the day. But at night I search for prey. I am a yellowish brown or gray color. I can grow to be four feet long.

©2000 The Education Center, Inc. • *Investigating Science • Amphibians and Reptiles* • TEC1741 • Key p. 48

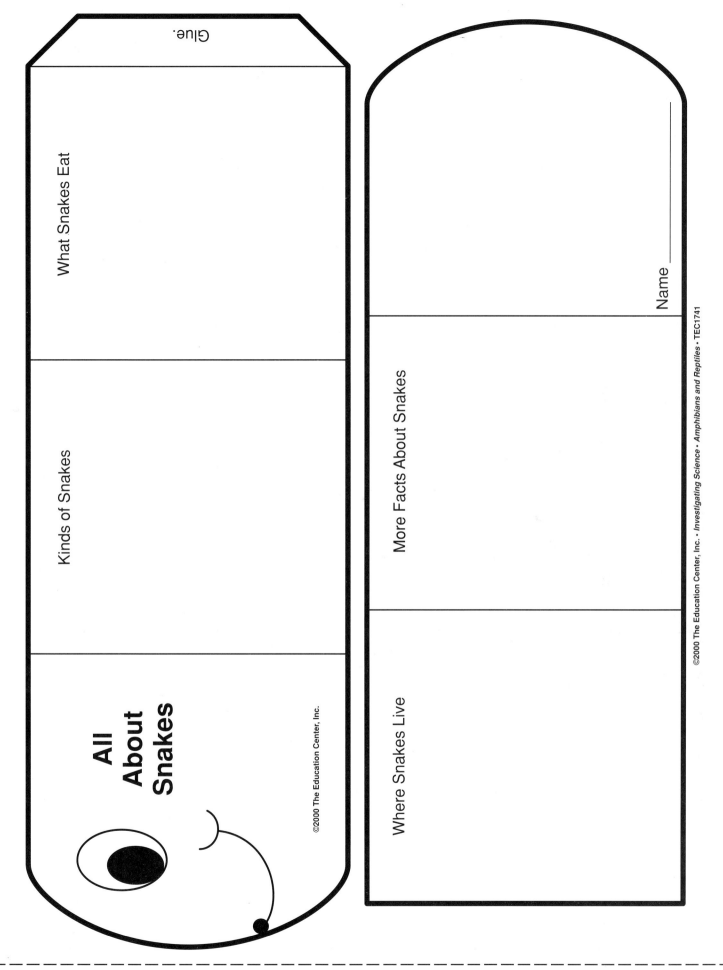

Glue.

What Snakes Eat

Kinds of Snakes

All
About
Snakes

©2000 The Education Center, Inc.

Name _____

More Facts About Snakes

Where Snakes Live

©2000 The Education Center, Inc. • *Investigating Science • Amphibians and Reptiles* • TEC1741

Note to the teacher: Use with "Winding Down" on page 20.

23

Lizards

Leaping lizards! Thrill and amaze your students with this collection of fun and creative lizard activities.

Lizards Around the World
(Reading, Matching, Geography)

Introduce your students to one lizard's adventure by reading aloud *Lizard Sees the World* by Susan Tews (Clarion Books, 1997). This wonderful tale introduces your children to Lizard, who is not content just sitting at home catching flies. Instead, he wants to see the world. Lizard soon finds out that curiosity and determination can take you far.

After reading the story, explain to your students that lizards live in many places throughout the world. In fact, they can be found on every continent except Antarctica. Introduce your students to a variety of interesting lizards and the countries in which they live by using the following matching and map activity. Give each student a copy of page 25. Instruct each student to cut out each lizard box at the bottom of the page. Then, one at a time, read aloud each lizard's name and the country in which it lives. Then guide each student in gluing each lizard box to the appropriate box on the map.

Amazing Lizard Literature

Amazing Lizards by Fay Robinson (Scholastic Inc., 1999)

Chameleons Are Cool by Martin Jenkins (Candlewick Press, 1998)

Frogs, Toads, Lizards, and Salamanders by Nancy Winslow Parker and Joan Richards Wright (Greenwillow Books, 1990)

The Iguana Brothers: A Tale of Two Lizards by Tony Johnston (The Blue Sky Press, 1995)

Komodo! by Peter Sis (Greenwillow Books, 1993)

Scholastic's The Magic School Bus®: Liz Looks for a Home by Tracey West (Scholastic Inc., 1998)

Snakes and Such by Alvin and Virginia Silverstein and Laura Silverstein Nunn (Twenty-First Century Books, 1999)

Background for the Teacher

- Lizards are closely related to snakes.
- Unlike snakes, lizards generally have two pairs of legs, external ear openings, and eyelids that open and close.
- Lizards have dry, scaly bodies.
- There are more than 3,000 different kinds of lizards.
- Lizards live on every continent except Antarctica.
- Periodically a lizard will shed its skin in patches.
- Lizards have teeth.
- Lizards use their tongues to help them smell.
- To defend themselves, some lizards puff up, hiss, open their mouths, or lash their tails.

Lively Lizards!
(Making a Booklet)

Use the following bookmaking activity to increase your students' knowledge of lizards. Supply each student with the materials listed. Then guide the student through the steps below to create her booklet.

Materials for each student: 1 copy each of pages 26–29, four 8" x 12" sheets of light-colored construction paper, glue, scissors, crayons, stapler

Steps:

1. Cut out each illustrated box on page 26.
2. Read page 27 carefully. Find the three missing illustrations and glue them onto page 27.
3. Read page 28 carefully. Find the three missing illustrations and glue them onto page 28.
4. Read page 29 carefully. Find the three missing illustrations and glue them onto page 29.
5. Cut along the bold borders on pages 27, 28, and 29. Then glue each page onto a separate sheet of construction paper.
6. Title the remaining sheet of construction paper "Lively Lizards." Draw pictures of lizards around the title.
7. To create the booklet, stack the sheets of construction paper with the "Lively Lizards" page on top. Then secure by stapling along the left-hand side.

Name _____

Lizards Around the World

©2000 The Education Center, Inc. • *Investigating Science • Amphibians and Reptiles* • TEC1741 • Key p. 48

Indonesia	Madagascar	Southwest United States	Southeast Asia	Central and South America	Australia	Europe
Komodo Dragon	Chameleon	Gila Monster	Tokay Gecko	Common Iguana	Australian Frilled Lizard	Worm Lizard

Note to the teacher: Use with "Lizards Around the World" on page 24.

Lizard Patterns
Use with "Lively Lizards!" on page 24.

Rhinoceros Iguana

Western Banded Gecko

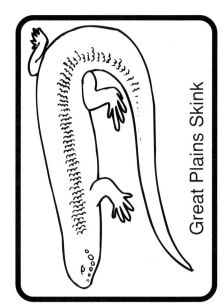

Great Plains Skink

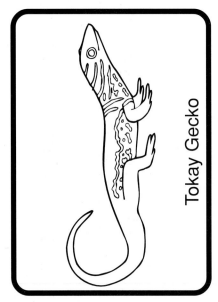

Tokay Gecko

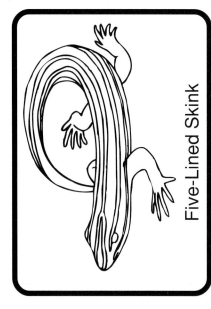

Five-Lined Skink

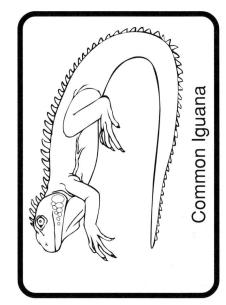

Common Iguana

Western Skink

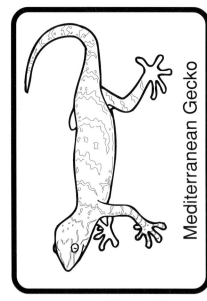

Mediterranean Gecko

Marine Iguana

©2000 The Education Center, Inc. • Investigating Science • Amphibians and Reptiles • TEC1741

Geckos

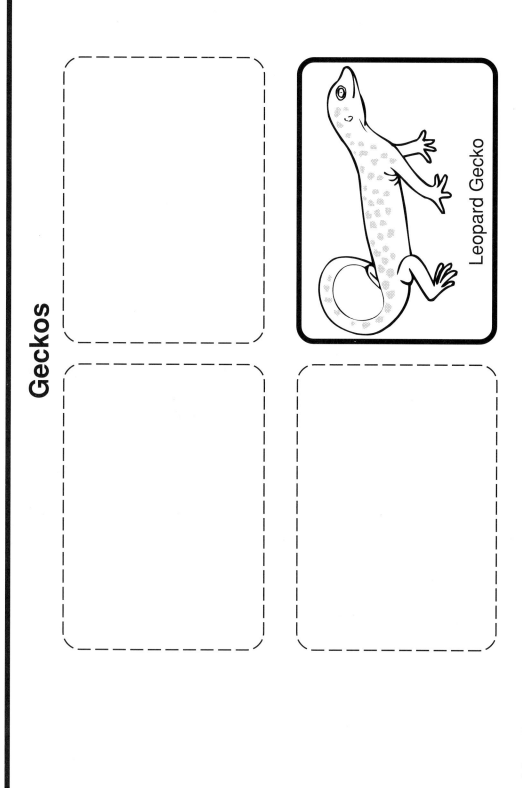

Leopard Gecko

Most lizards are quiet animals, but not the gecko! This lizard makes a loud noise that sounds like the word *gecko*. Geckos are fun to watch, but they don't like to be handled. Geckos can get quite large. The Tokay gecko can get up to one foot in length. Geckos love insects. They can eat as many as 200 cockroaches in one day! Most geckos are *nocturnal* (active at night), but some are *diurnal* (active during the day). Some live in trees and some live on land.

©2000 The Education Center, Inc. • *Investigating Science* • *Amphibians and Reptiles* • TEC1741 • Key p. 48

Note to the teacher: Use with "Lively Lizards!" on page 24.

Skinks

Skinks have shiny, smooth, and flat scales that overlap. They also have short legs and pointed snouts, or noses. Skinks mostly live in tropical and mild regions, but some live in North America too. Skinks love to eat small insects. They do not get much bigger than 16 inches long. Skinks' legs are not very strong, and they move slower than other lizards. Skinks are often seen under houses, in gardens, and around compost piles. Gardeners like skinks because they are a good way to control insects in the garden.

Broad-Headed Skink

Note to the teacher: Use with "Lively Lizards!" on page 24.

Iguanas

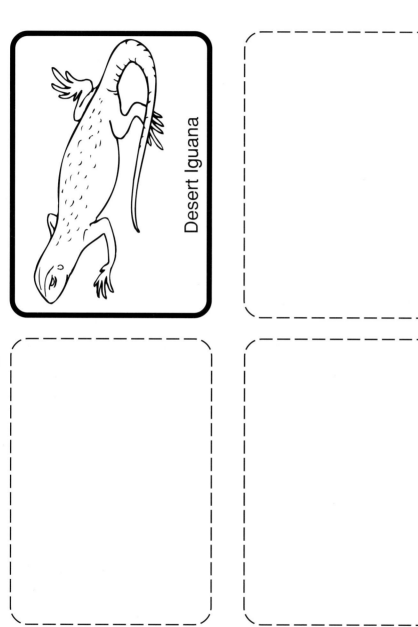

Desert Iguana

Iguanas are the most popular pet reptile in the United States. Iguanas are native to Central and South America and the Caribbean Islands. They live in trees but also do well on land. Iguanas have long, sharp claws perfect for climbing trees. If an iguana falls from a branch, it will land feetfirst just like a cat. Iguanas are good swimmers too. An iguana can stay underwater for 30 minutes! Iguanas are *diurnal* reptiles. They need to be in the sun to stay healthy. Iguanas can have a life span of 20 years or more.

©2000 The Education Center, Inc. • *Investigating Science* • Amphibians and Reptiles • TEC1741 • Key p. 48

Note to the teacher: Use with "Lively Lizards!" on page 24.

Salamanders & Newts

This unit is just what you need to help your students learn more about the secret, slimy, and slippery world of salamanders and newts.

Similar but Different
(Compare and Contrast, Research)

Looks like a lizard. Moves like a lizard. Must be a lizard. Wrong! Use the following activity to help your students discover the differences between lizards and salamanders. Share several books on salamanders and lizards with your students (see the booklist below and the lizard booklist on page 24). Then have your students help you brainstorm a list of similarities and differences between the two types of creatures. Divide a large sheet of chart paper into two columns. Head one column "Lizards" and head the other column "Salamanders." Then list the students' brainstormed responses in the appropriate column. Next, divide your students into pairs. Give each pair one copy of page 32. Direct the pair to complete the chart on page 32 by using the information listed on the class chart. Also allow pairs to use encyclopedias and other references on salamanders and lizards to help them complete the chart. To culminate the activity, have volunteers from various groups give their responses to the different boxes on page 32. If desired, use the following bulletin board display idea to showcase each pair's completed chart. Enlarge one of the lizard patterns on page 26 and one of the salamander patterns on page 34; then color each pattern appropriately. Next, post each pattern in the upper right- and left-hand corners of a bulletin board titled "Similar but Different." Then arrange the completed charts on the board for all to enjoy.

Names **Sally, Mandy**   Compare/Contrast

Similar but Different

Lizards   Salamanders

Similarities

Most lizards and all salamanders have tails. Usually they both have four feet and crawl on the ground. Most salamanders and lizards are carnivores. They are both cold-blooded animals and are vertebrates.

Differences

Lizards		Salamanders
Lizards can live in or near water, but many can live in hot, dry places.	Habitat	Salamanders live in cool, damp places.
Lizards have claws.	Feet	Salamanders do not have claws.
A lizard's skin is rough and scaly.	Skin	A salamander's skin is smooth.
Some lizards can grow to 10 feet long.	Size	Salamanders range in size from 1 inch to 5 feet.
Lizards are reptiles.	Animal Group (Amphibian or Reptile?)	Salamanders are amphibians.

Background for the Teacher

- Salamanders are amphibians.
- Salamanders have thin, smooth skin like frogs.
- Salamanders avoid the sun and live in cool, damp places.
- Salamanders drink through their skin. They soak up the water they need through their skin.
- Salamanders eat earthworms, slugs, spiders, and insects. Large salamanders may eat small snakes, baby mice, and small frogs.
- Many salamanders hibernate during the winter.
- About 380 varieties of salamanders have been identified.
- All salamanders have tails.
- Salamanders range in length from one inch to five feet.

Super Salamander and Noteworthy Newt Books

Newt by Matt Novak (HarperTrophy, 1997)
Salamanders by Emery and Durga Bernhard (Holiday House, Inc.; 1995)
Shy Salamanders by D. M. Souza (Carolrhoda Books, Inc.; 1994)
The Salamander Room by Anne Mazer (Alfred A. Knopf, Inc.; 1994)
What Newt Could Do for Turtle by Jonathan London (Candlewick Press, 1998)

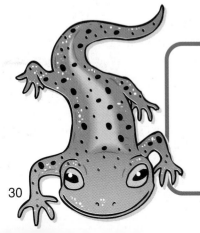

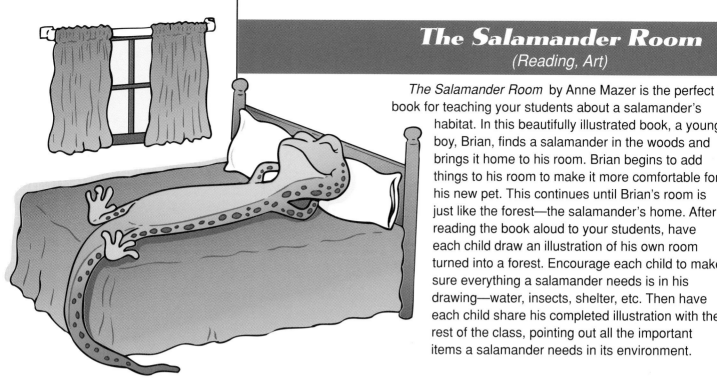

The Salamander Room
(Reading, Art)

The Salamander Room by Anne Mazer is the perfect book for teaching your students about a salamander's habitat. In this beautifully illustrated book, a young boy, Brian, finds a salamander in the woods and brings it home to his room. Brian begins to add things to his room to make it more comfortable for his new pet. This continues until Brian's room is just like the forest—the salamander's home. After reading the book aloud to your students, have each child draw an illustration of his own room turned into a forest. Encourage each child to make sure everything a salamander needs is in his drawing—water, insects, shelter, etc. Then have each child share his completed illustration with the rest of the class, pointing out all the important items a salamander needs in its environment.

Splendid Salamanders and Nifty Newts
(Art, Making a Booklet, Research)

Introduce your students to the colorful world of salamanders and newts with the following booklet-making and research activity. Give each student one copy each of pages 33 and 34, scissors, and crayons. First, direct each student to write her name on the blank at the top of page 33. Next, instruct the student to follow the directions in each section of pages 33 and 34 to guide her in coloring each illustration. Once the student has colored each illustration, direct her to cut out each section and the title page along the bold lines. Instruct the student to stack the sections with the title page on top; then staple the booklet together along the left-hand side.

Further challenge each student to learn more about one of the salamanders in her booklet. Give each student one copy of the graphic organizer on page 35. Then tell each student to choose one salamander in her booklet to research. Provide students with a variety of books on salamanders and newts. Then have each student research her chosen salamander and record her findings on page 35. After students have collected and recorded their findings, have each student show the class the colored illustration of her chosen salamander from her booklet and read aloud the information recorded on her graphic organizer. If desired, display all the graphic organizers on a bulletin board titled "Splendid Salamanders and Nifty Newts."

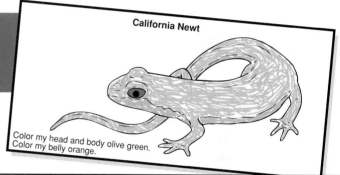

California Newt

Color my head and body olive green.
Color my belly orange.

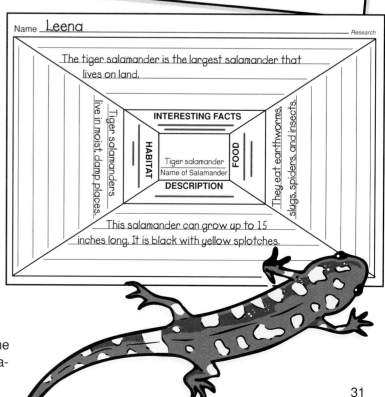

Name Leena

Research

The tiger salamander is the largest salamander that lives on land.

INTERESTING FACTS

HABITAT — Tiger salamanders live in moist, damp places.

FOOD — They eat earthworms, slugs, spiders, and insects.

Tiger salamander
Name of Salamander

DESCRIPTION — This salamander can grow up to 15 inches long. It is black with yellow splotches.

Similar but Different

Lizards   ### Salamanders

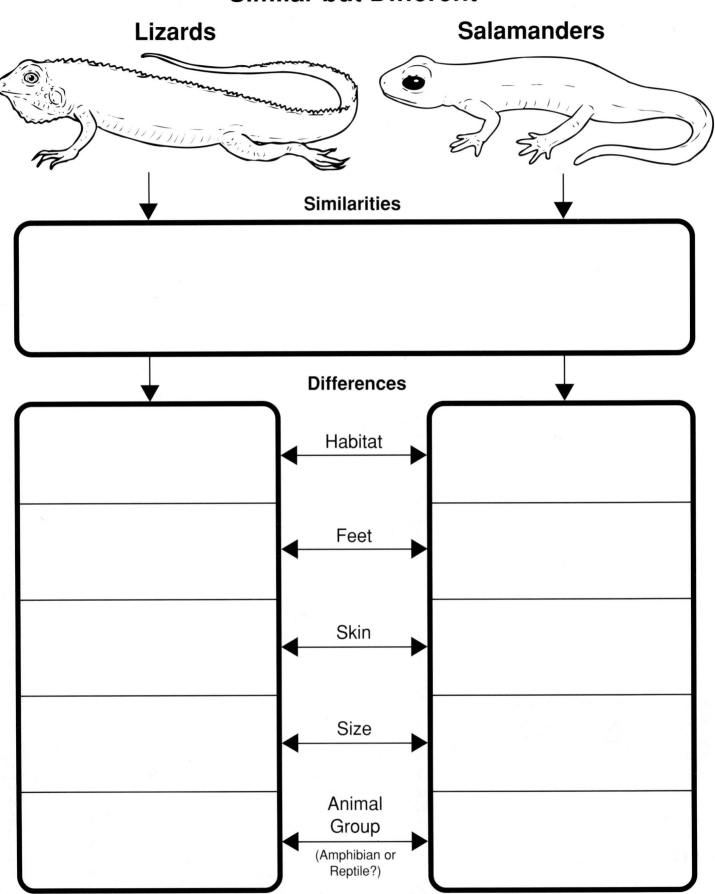

Similarities

Differences

Habitat

Feet

Skin

Size

Animal
Group
(Amphibian or
Reptile?)

©2000 The Education Center, Inc. • *Investigating Science* • *Amphibians and Reptiles* • TEC1741 • Key p. 30

32   **Note to the teacher:** Use with "Similar but Different" on page 30.

Splendid Salamanders and Nifty Newts

Name: _____

Spotted Salamander

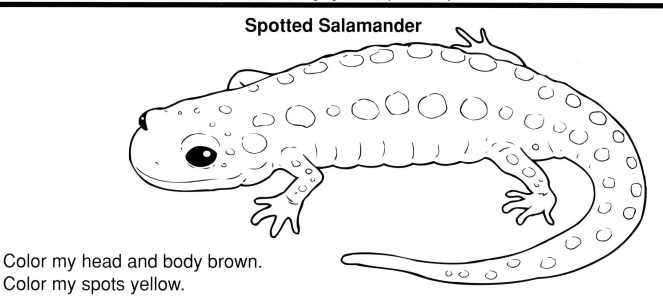

Color my head and body brown.
Color my spots yellow.

Marbled Salamander

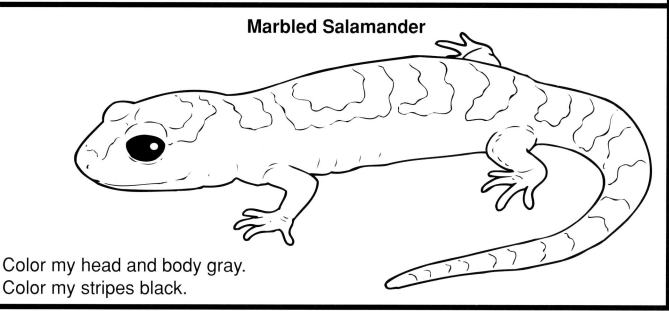

Color my head and body gray.
Color my stripes black.

Patterns

Use with "Splendid Salamanders and Nifty Newts" on page 31.

Fire Salamander

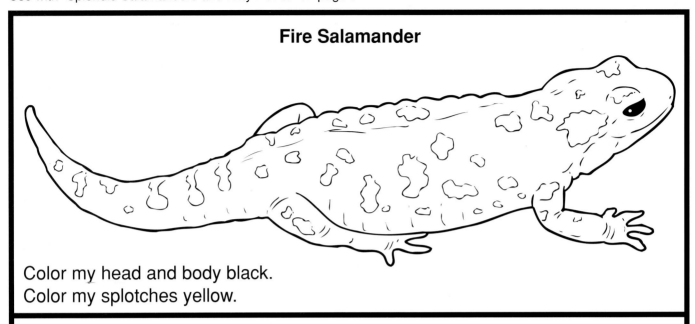

Color my head and body black.
Color my splotches yellow.

California Newt

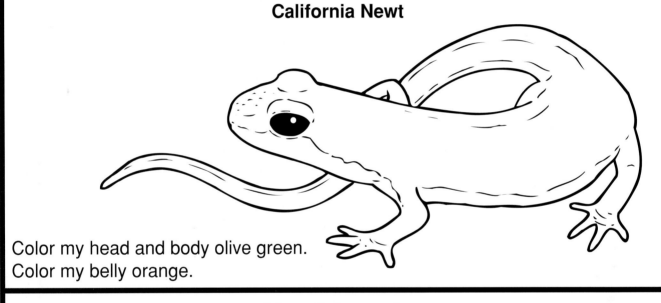

Color my head and body olive green.
Color my belly orange.

Tiger Salamander

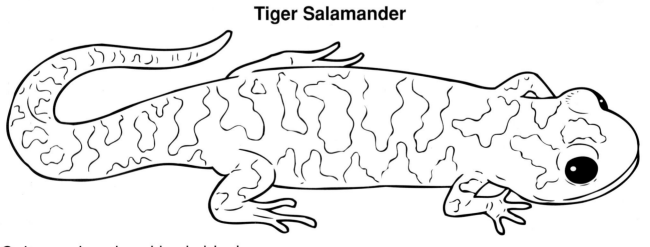

Color my head and body black.
Color my splotches yellow.

Name

INTERESTING FACTS
Write interesting or unusual facts about
your salamander.

FOOD
Describe what your
salamander eats.

Name of Salamander

DESCRIPTION
Include facts on its size and color.

HABITAT
Describe your salamander's
habitat.

Note to the teacher: Use with "Splendid Salamanders and Nifty Newts" on page 31.

Turtles

Turtles may move slowly, but your youngsters' learning will speed right along when they dive into these fascinating turtle-related learning activities.

Turtle Types
(Research, Graphic Organizer, Presentation)

Approximately 250 species of turtles exist! So how do you begin to discover these many varieties with your youngsters? This small-group research project will help you narrow your investigation to seven turtle types. In advance, draw seven large graphic organizers on bulletin board paper (similar to the one shown, but with category headings only). Using the list on this page, label each poster with a different turtle type. Gather a large supply of books and research material relating to turtles or specific types of turtles. Divide your students into seven groups and give each group a poster. Encourage each group to research and collaborate to gather and write information for each area on the graphic organizer. Encourage each group to collect or draw pictures of its turtle type, too. Display the completed posters in your classroom and provide an opportunity for each group to share its findings!

Background for the Teacher

- About 250 different species of turtles are known to exist within seven main groups: mud and musk turtles, pond and marsh turtles, sea turtles, side-necked turtles, snapping turtles, soft-shelled turtles, and tortoises.
- A turtle is the only reptile that has a shell.
- Most turtles can pull their legs, tail, and head inside their shell when threatened.
- Turtles have no teeth; instead, a sharp-edged beak helps them cut their food.
- Turtles' legs and feet vary with their environment. Land turtles have short stubby legs. Freshwater turtles have webbed feet and longer legs. Sea turtles' legs are more like flippers.
- After laying her egg or eggs, a female turtle buries them and doesn't return, leaving young hatchlings to survive on their own.
- Turtles' diets vary among species, but most can eat plants and small animals and insects.

Turtle Types

mud and musk turtles	snapping turtles
pond and marsh turtles	soft-shelled turtles
sea turtles	tortoises
side-necked turtles	

Turtle Tales

Follow the Moon by Sarah Weeks (HarperCollins Children's Books, 1995)

Shy Little Turtle by Howard Goldsmith (McGraw-Hill, 1998)

The Foolish Tortoise by Richard Buckley (Little Simon, 1998)

The Great Turtle Drive by Steve Sanfield (Alfred A. Knopf, Inc.; 1996)

Turtle Bay by Saviour Pirotta (Farrar, Straus & Giroux, Inc.; 1997)

Sea Turtles graphic organizer:

Food
- sea grass
- crabs
- jellyfish

Home
- stay in the sea but come up for air

Shell
- flat for swimming
- can't pull head inside
- leatherbacks have skin instead of a hard shell

Size
- largest turtles

Speed
- fast! up to 20 miles per hour

Eggs
- females come on land to lay eggs
- lay about 100 eggs

Danger
- animals dig up eggs and eat them
- sharks attack
- people hunting

Legs/Feet
- legs look like flippers

Other
- five kinds of sea turtles in the U.S.

Protective Packaging
(Demonstration, Experiment)

Simulate a turtle shell's protective nature with this demonstration. In advance, gather several raw eggs; a palm-sized rock; a large transparent, contained work area (an unbreakable plastic storage container); several paper plates; and a variety of containers and coverings, such as a plastic margarine tub, small metal bowl, small cardboard box, six-inch circle of cloth or flexible plastic, etc. (Each item should be able to cover and surround an egg.) Place one egg on a paper plate in the work area. Ask your students to predict what will happen if you drop the rock on the unprotected egg. Drop the rock atop the egg from a few inches above and allow students to observe the results. Remove the damaged egg, plate, and rock; then place another egg and plate in the work area. Next, display several of the containers and ask students to suggest a way to protect the egg from the next drop, such as inverting a margarine tub atop the egg. Drop the rock on the chosen protective covering; then lift the protective layer to examine the egg. Record the covering and the condition of the egg on a chart. Allow students to experiment with several of the coverings provided. (Be sure to provide some that may not protect against the rock's fall.) Conclude the demonstration by explaining that a turtle's body is fragile like the egg, but its shell protects it from animal attacks and other dangerous encounters.

Turtle Anatomy
(Investigation)

Help your students discover the unique bone structure of a turtle with this anatomy activity. Give each child a copy of "Flexible Features" on page 39. Discuss the bone structure of the turtle shown with exposed legs, head, and tail. Using the coloring code and labels, encourage each child to color the appropriate sections of this turtle. Next, ask each child to study the turtle that has withdrawn its extremities into the shell. Point out the new positions of many of the bones, such as the neck and tail portions of the backbone. Ask each child to locate the bone structures in their new positions and color them using the code. The colored areas on both diagrams will clearly display the flexibility of a turtle's spine. (Note: Side-necked turtles retract their heads differently than shown in this diagram. Encourage your students to research the anatomy characteristics of this unique species in "Turtle Types" on page 36.)

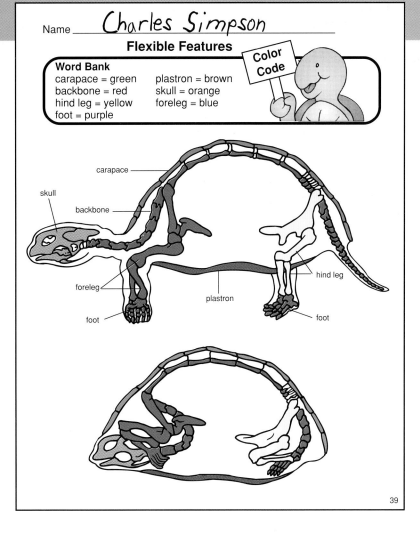

Name __Charles Simpson__

Flexible Features

Color Code

Word Bank
carapace = green
backbone = red
hind leg = yellow
foot = purple
plastron = brown
skull = orange
foreleg = blue

carapace

skull

backbone

foreleg

plastron

foot

hind leg

foot

39

Turtle Tambourine
(Arts and Crafts, Music)

Shake up your study of turtles with this clever craft creation.

Materials for one tambourine:
— one 6" Styrofoam® bowl
— 1 green poster board copy of the pattern on page 40
— 1" squares of brown and green tissue paper
— access to diluted glue mixture (¹/₂ white glue, ¹/₂ water)
— paintbrush
— 10 beans
— white glue (undiluted)
— 2 wiggle eyes
— scissors

Steps:
1. To create a turtle shell, use the diluted glue mixture to paint overlapping tissue paper squares onto the bowl's convex side. Let it dry.
2. Cut out the turtle pattern along the heavy solid outlines.
3. Place the cutout on a flat surface and set the beans in the middle of the shape.
4. Draw a line of glue near the outer edge of the turtle's body as shown.
5. Align the bowl over the cutout and hold it in place to seal the edges. Let it dry completely.
6. Glue the wiggle eyes to the turtle's head.
7. Carefully bend the four legs down.

Tap your turtle tambourine on each X while you recite this turtle chant!
I am a turtle, (X X)
Steady and slow. (X X)
I move with patience (X X)
Wherever I go. (X X)

If I'm in danger, (X X)
My shell helps me hide. (X X)
I tuck my head (X X)
And legs inside. (X X)

Turtle Estimation
(Math)

Endless estimation possibilities abound when you combine turtle facts with this important math skill.

Display an eight-foot-long bulletin board cutout of a simply drawn loggerhead turtle. Also provide other varieties of turtle cutouts in their approximate sizes.

Ask children to identify everyday objects that are about the same length as the loggerhead and other turtles displayed. Conclude the activity by giving each child a copy of "Turtle Estimation" on page 41 to complete independently. What a way to size up your turtle investigations!

Flexible Features

Word Bank

carapace = green	plastron = brown
backbone = red	skull = orange
hind leg = yellow	foreleg = blue
foot = purple	

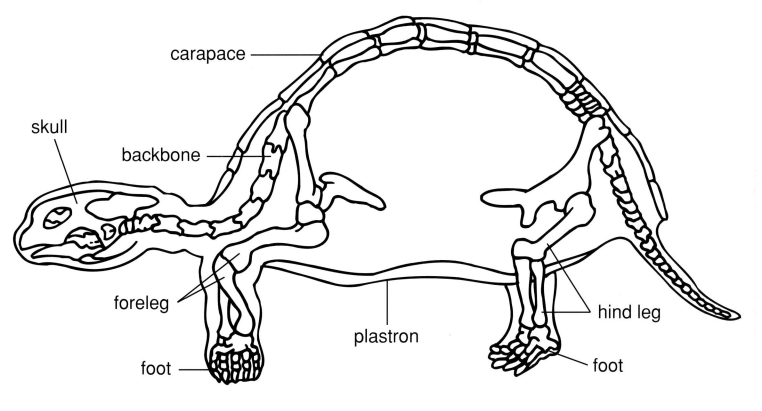

carapace

skull

backbone

foreleg

foot

plastron

hind leg

foot

Turtle Pattern
Use with "Turtle Tambourine" on page 38.

Name _____

Turtle Estimation

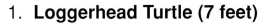

Estimate the length of each turtle.
Color the circle for the object that is closest to the turtle's length.

1. **Loggerhead Turtle (7 feet)**

○ pencil   ○ bus
○ car   ○ cat

2. **Musk Turtle (5 inches)**

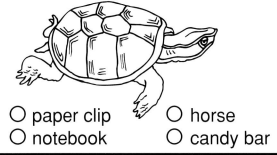

○ paper clip   ○ horse
○ notebook   ○ candy bar

3. **Box Turtle (7 inches)**

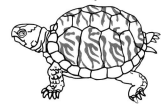

○ sheet of paper   ○ baseball bat
○ pencil   ○ house

4. **Mud Turtle (3 inches)**

○ swimming pool   ○ crayon
○ television   ○ toaster

5. **Leatherback Turtle (8 feet)**

○ car   ○ telephone
○ computer   ○ cookie

6. **Painted Turtle (10 inches)**

○ shoebox   ○ eraser
○ table   ○ glue bottle

7. **Ridley Turtle (27 inches)**

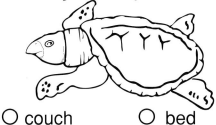

○ couch   ○ bed
○ cupcake   ○ television

8. **Snapping Turtle (18 inches)**

○ lunchbox   ○ sandwich
○ whale   ○ backpack

Bonus Box: Color the longest and the shortest turtles.

Alligators and Crocodiles

To better understand some of nature's oldest reptiles, let your youngsters sink their teeth into the following activities and reproducibles.

Who Am I?
(Comparing)

How can you tell an alligator from a crocodile? Just look at its nose! Use the following comparison activity to introduce your students to the differences and similarities of these reptile relatives. Begin by sharing several nonfiction books on alligators and crocodiles with your students (see list below). Then brainstorm with your children a list of interesting alligator and crocodile facts. Record their ideas on chart paper. Next, give each child a copy of page 45, one 18" x 12" sheet of construction paper, scissors, glue, and crayons. Instruct each child to cut out the alligator and crocodile patterns and glue them onto her construction paper as shown. Then have her cut out each fact card. Direct the child to study the similarities and differences of the two reptile illustrations. Then have her read each fact card carefully and glue it under the correct reptile as shown. Next, have the child use the class chart information to help her fill in the two fact cards that ask for similarities and then glue one card under each reptile. Finally, have each child color the alligator and crocodile illustrations. Hang the finished products on a bulletin board titled "Who Am I?"

Reptile Reads

Alligators (Early Bird Nature Books series) by Frank J. Staub (Lerner Publications Company, 1995)

An Extraordinary Egg by Leo Lionni (Alfred A. Knopf, Inc.; 1994)

Crocodiles and Alligators by Seymour Simon (HarperCollins Children's Books, 1999)

The Crocodile Family Book by Mark Deeble (North-South Books Inc., 1994)

Imagine You Are a Crocodile by Karen Wallace and Mike Bostock (Henry Holt and Company, 1997)

Background for the Teacher

Similarities:

Alligators and crocodiles...
- have been around since the time of the dinosaurs
- are semiaquatic, living on land and in water
- can survive for nearly two years without a meal
- will eat almost any animal, but generally prey on small rodents, birds, and fish

Differences:
- Alligators have short, wide snouts.
- Crocodiles have long, pointed snouts; flat foreheads; and clearly visible teeth when their mouths are closed.
- There are two kinds of alligators: the Chinese and the American.
- There are 14 kinds of crocodiles found in Africa, Australia, Asia, North and South America, and some western Pacific Islands.
- Some alligators can grow to 12 feet long and weigh 500 pounds.
- Crocodiles vary in size, from 5 to 20 feet long, and some can weigh a ton or more.

Crocodile Hats
(Vocabulary, Art)

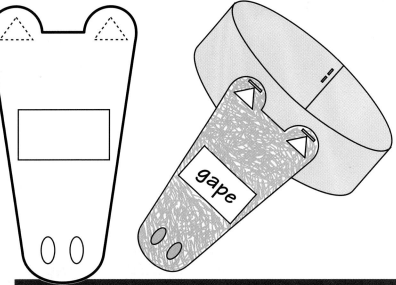

Turn your youngsters into crocodile experts with this fun vocabulary-building activity. Make an enlarged photocopy of the crocodile face pattern shown; then make a copy for each student. Next, make a photocopy of the Crocodile Vocabulary Box below for each student. Discuss the words and their meanings with your students. Next, provide each child with a green crayon, a black marker, one 9" x 12" sheet of green construction paper, one sentence strip, scissors, and tape. Then follow the steps below to help each student create his own cool crocodile vocabulary hat.

To review the important crocodile vocabulary, have students wear their cool croc hats as you call on volunteers to stand and share their words and definitions with the class.

Steps:
1. Color the crocodile face green and cut it out. Choose one vocabulary word to write in the box on the crocodile's snout.
2. Trace the crocodile's snout onto the green construction paper and cut it out. Then write the definition of the vocabulary word on the green paper cutout.
3. Tape the top portion of the green paper cutout to the underside of the crocodile's snout so the definition faces up.
4. Staple the top of the crocodile head to the center of the sentence strip.
5. Cut along the dotted lines to make eye-holes.
6. Size the hat to fit the student by wrapping the sentence strip around his head. Remove the hat and secure in place by stapling.

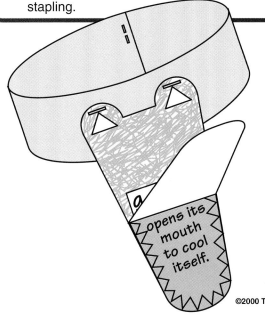

Crocodile Counting
(Reading, Math)

Continue your students' learning about crocodiles and reinforce their counting skills by sharing the story *Counting Crocodiles* by Judy Sierra (Harcourt Brace & Company, 1997). To further enjoy this tale, create a display where students can count crocs just like the monkey! First cover a bulletin board with blue paper. Next, hang a yellow circle labeled "Lemon Island" in the bottom left-hand corner. Then title the bulletin board "Count Us, Please!" and attach a yellow circle labeled "Banana Island" to the top right-hand corner of the board. Pair students and assign each pair a counting group of crocodiles from the story (for example: one crocodile with a big smile, two crocs resting on rocks, three crocs rocking in a box, etc.). Have the pair illustrate its assigned crocodile scene on a sheet of white paper. Hang each scene (in numerical order) on the board. Connect the scenes to the islands with brown string to indicate the monkey's path. As a concluding activity, challenge students to count the number of crocodiles the monkey encountered going to *(55)* and from *(55)* Banana Island *(a total of 110)*.

Crocodile Vocabulary Box

reptiles: animals with scaly skin that crawl on their stomachs or creep along on short legs

cold-blooded: having a body temperature that stays the same as the air and surfaces around it

bask: to lie in a warm place

gape: the way a crocodile keeps its mouth open to cool down

semiaquatic: frequenting, but not living entirely in water

predators: animals that hunt other animals for food

prey: an animal that is hunted for food

Egyptian plover: a small bird that picks food from a crocodile's teeth

swallow: how a crocodile eats food without chewing

bellow: to make a loud, deep sound like a roar

clutch: a litter of crocodile eggs

hatchlings: baby animals that have just hatched from eggs

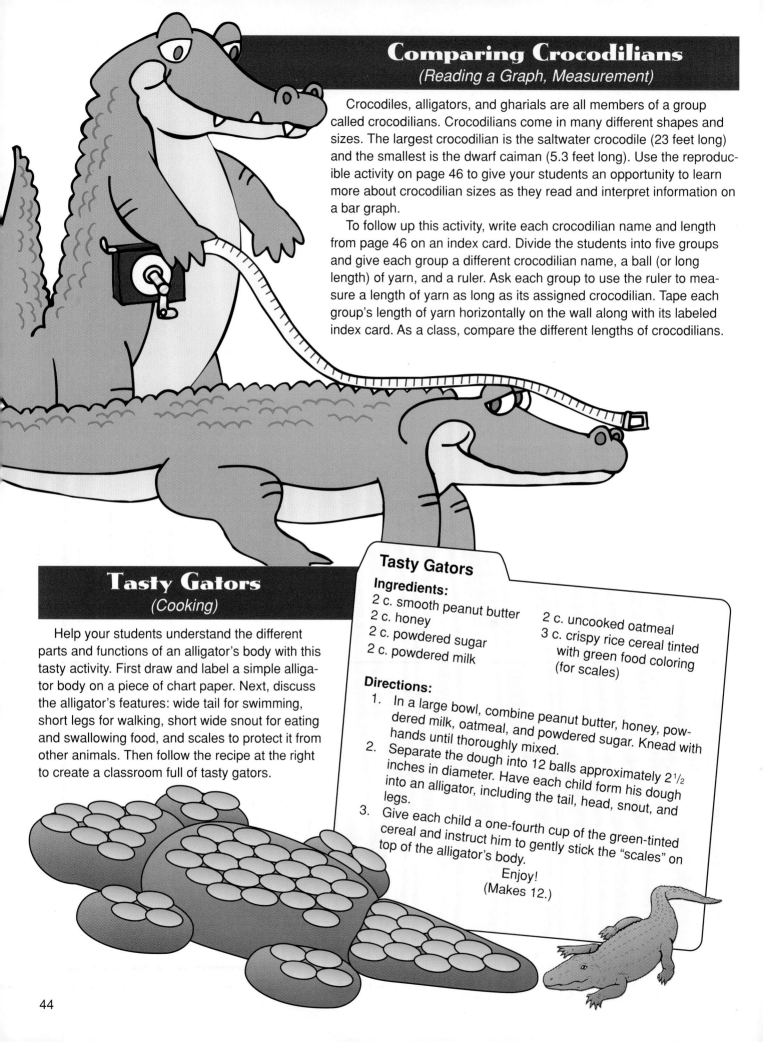

Comparing Crocodilians
(Reading a Graph, Measurement)

Crocodiles, alligators, and gharials are all members of a group called crocodilians. Crocodilians come in many different shapes and sizes. The largest crocodilian is the saltwater crocodile (23 feet long) and the smallest is the dwarf caiman (5.3 feet long). Use the reproducible activity on page 46 to give your students an opportunity to learn more about crocodilian sizes as they read and interpret information on a bar graph.

To follow up this activity, write each crocodilian name and length from page 46 on an index card. Divide the students into five groups and give each group a different crocodilian name, a ball (or long length) of yarn, and a ruler. Ask each group to use the ruler to measure a length of yarn as long as its assigned crocodilian. Tape each group's length of yarn horizontally on the wall along with its labeled index card. As a class, compare the different lengths of crocodilians.

Tasty Gators
(Cooking)

Help your students understand the different parts and functions of an alligator's body with this tasty activity. First draw and label a simple alligator body on a piece of chart paper. Next, discuss the alligator's features: wide tail for swimming, short legs for walking, short wide snout for eating and swallowing food, and scales to protect it from other animals. Then follow the recipe at the right to create a classroom full of tasty gators.

Tasty Gators

Ingredients:
2 c. smooth peanut butter
2 c. honey
2 c. powdered sugar
2 c. powdered milk
2 c. uncooked oatmeal
3 c. crispy rice cereal tinted with green food coloring (for scales)

Directions:
1. In a large bowl, combine peanut butter, honey, powdered milk, oatmeal, and powdered sugar. Knead with hands until thoroughly mixed.
2. Separate the dough into 12 balls approximately 2½ inches in diameter. Have each child form his dough into an alligator, including the tail, head, snout, and legs.
3. Give each child a one-fourth cup of the green-tinted cereal and instruct him to gently stick the "scales" on top of the alligator's body.
Enjoy!
(Makes 12.)

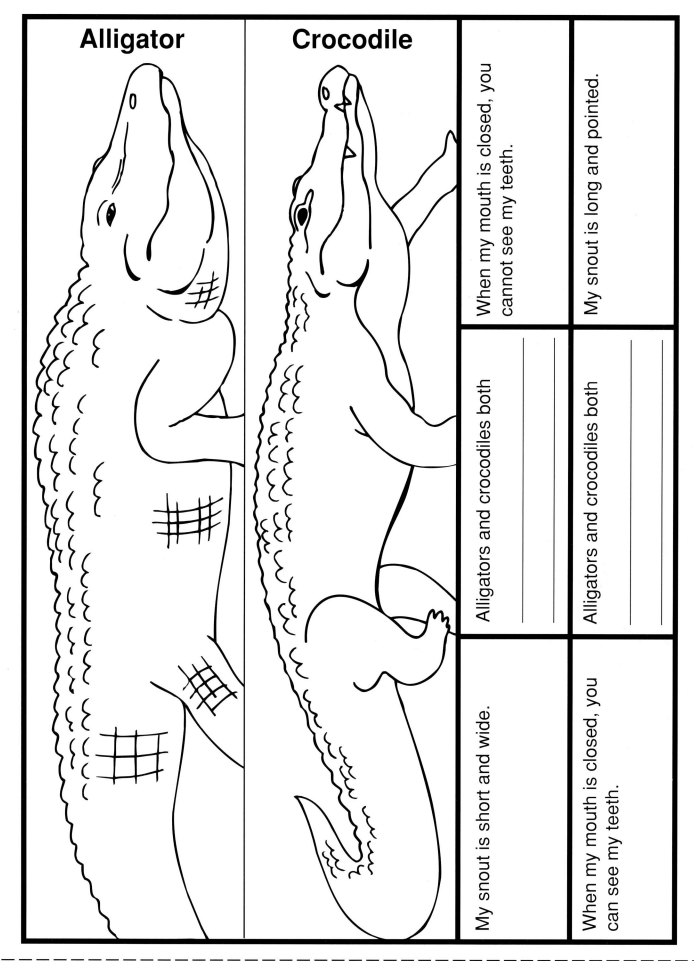

Alligator	Crocodile		
		When my mouth is closed, you cannot see my teeth.	My snout is long and pointed.
		Alligators and crocodiles both _____	Alligators and crocodiles both _____
		My snout is short and wide.	When my mouth is closed, you can see my teeth.

Comparing Crocodilians

Approximate length in feet

25
20
15
10
5
0

| American alligator | Dwarf crocodile | Gharial | Saltwater crocodile | Nile crocodile |

Answer the questions.
Use the graph.

1. Which kind of crocodile is 23 feet long? _____

2. Which two crocodilians are longer than the Nile crocodile? _____

   _____

3. How long is the gharial? _____

4. Which kind of crocodile is almost the same size as the American alligator? _____

   _____

5. Which kind of crocodile is just over 6 feet long? _____

6. How many feet longer is the saltwater crocodile than the dwarf crocodile? _____

   _____

7. Which crocodile is longer than the American alligator and smaller than the gharial? _____

8. Do you think the saltwater crocodile weighs more than the American alligator?
   _____ Why? _____

   _____

Greater-Than Gators

Trace the signs.

| greater than | less than | equal to |

Write >, <, or = in each circle.

9 ◯ 13	0 ◯ 1	20 ◯ 4
10 ◯ 20	17 ◯ 17	12 ◯ 9
49 ◯ 50	96 ◯ 35	15 ◯ 70
15 ◯ 25	21 ◯ 27	82 ◯ 82
13 ◯ 10	16 ◯ 86	37 ◯ 42
12 ◯ 24	5 ◯ 15	70 ◯ 69
7 ◯ 7	31 ◯ 17	61 ◯ 61
90 ◯ 89	100 ◯ 89	48 ◯ 51

Note to the teacher: Have each child check his work by drawing teeth in the signs. The alligator should always "eat" the bigger number.

Answer Keys

Page 6
Amphibians:
Tree Toad
Tiger Salamander
Green Tree Frog
European Common Frog
Marine Toad
Fire Salamander
Poison-Dart Frog
African Bullfrog
Wood Frog
Spadefoot Toad
California Newt
Spring Peeper

Reptiles:
Gila Monster
Western Diamondback Rattlesnake
Tuatara
Leatherback Turtle
Giant Galapagos Tortoise
Gecko
Flying Dragon
American Alligator
Chameleon
Rough Green Snake
Garter Snake
Spotted Turtle

Page 11
Answers will vary. Possible answers are listed below.
How do they breathe?
A: They breathe through lungs, skin, or both.
R: They breathe with lungs.
Where do they live?
A: They usually live in or near water.
R: They live in a variety of environments both in and out of water.
How do they move?
A: Most move on four legs. Some hop.
R: Most move on four legs, except snakes and some lizards.
What do they eat?
A: Most eat meat, but some eat only plants.
R: Most eat meat, but a few lizards eat only plants.
Do they need to be in or near water?
A: Yes, most need water to keep their skin moist. Some need water to reproduce.
R: Some depend on water, but others live in a desert environment.
Do they lay eggs?
A: Most lay eggs. A few give birth to live young.
R: Most lay eggs. A few give birth to live young.

Page 16
1. A female frog lays eggs in the pond.
2. Soon a tadpole hatches from each egg.
3. First, the tadpole's back legs begin to sprout.
4. Next, the front legs start to appear.
5. Then the tail starts to disappear.
6. Now a frog is ready to come out of the water.

Page 22

Garter Snake
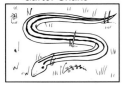

Cottonmouth

Corn Snake
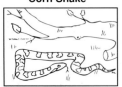

Green Snake

Rattlesnake

Water Snake

Page 25
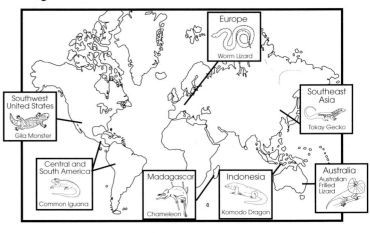

Pages 27, 28, and 29
Geckos: Leopard Gecko, Tokay Gecko, Mediterranean Gecko, Western Banded Gecko
Skinks: Broad-Headed Skink, Western Skink, Great Plains Skink, Five-Lined Skink
Iguanas: Desert Iguana, Rhinoceros Iguana, Common Iguana, Marine Iguana

Page 41
1. car
2. candy bar
3. pencil
4. crayon
5. car
6. shoebox
7. television
8. backpack
Bonus Box answer: The leatherback and the mudd turtle should be colored.

Page 46
1. saltwater crocodile
2. saltwater crocodile and gharial
3. 20 feet long
4. Nile crocodile
5. dwarf crocodile
6. 16 feet longer
7. Nile crocodile
8. Answers will vary. (It is reasonable to assume the saltwater crocodile will weigh more since it's much bigger.)

Page 47

9 < 13	0 < 1	20 > 4
10 < 20	17 = 17	12 > 9
49 < 50	96 > 35	15 < 70
15 < 25	21 < 27	82 = 82
13 > 10	16 < 86	37 < 42
12 < 24	5 < 15	70 > 69
7 = 7	31 > 17	61 = 61
90 > 89	100 > 89	48 < 51